THE SUGAR
KNOCKOUT

COOKBOOK

KERRI PAGLIARINI

THE SUGAR

KNOCKOUT

COOKBOOK

**CLEAN-EATING RECIPES TO
HELP CURB CRAVINGS &
BALANCE BLOOD SUGAR**

CONTENTS

0 / INTRO

DEFINITIVE GUIDE TO RECIPES THAT HARMONIZE BLOOD SUGAR & CURB SUGAR CRAVINGS.

My name is Kerri Pagliarini, and my journey to a healthier life wasn't paved with sugar.

As someone who battled sugar addiction and faced hormonal challenges, I understand the struggle of constantly being pulled towards sugary treats. It's easy to succumb, but the after-effects? Not so sweet.

There was a time in my life when my addiction took such a toll on my body that I found myself in the hospital, facing the need for surgery. That was the turning point—the wake-up call I needed.

I enrolled in the Institute for Integrative Nutrition to find answers and discovered that my health issues were caused by hormone imbalances—a byproduct of my diet.

When I addressed my nutrition, I not only got healthy, I *finally* conquered my sugar demons.

Armed with newfound knowledge and a passion for change, I began coaching women who, like me, were wrestling with hormonal imbalances...and soon discovered that many of them also had an intricate and often tumultuous relationship with sugar. That's when I shifted my focus to teach the art of letting go of sugar habits.

This book is for everyone ready to be free from sugar's whims.

It's not just about abstaining. It's about understanding the **why**, the **how**, and the **what** of sugar's impact on our bodies.

This book isn't just a collection of recipes. It's about celebrating life and rediscovering your vitality and joy through clean eating.

So, dear reader, as you flip through these pages, let the flavors and wholesome ingredients inspire you. Remember, every meal, every bite, and every choice is a step towards a life where you feel sexy, energized, and truly in control.

To a sweeter life, sans sugar.

KERRI PAGLIARINI

EMPOWER-WELLNESSCOACHING.COM

1 / TONICS

These simple morning elixirs that are designed to flush the liver, kidneys, and lymphs; support detox; improve absorption of minerals; encourage digestion; and break down fat. They may also help satisfy cravings.

LEMON CRAVINGS BLASTER

1 MIN · MAKES 1

1 cup room-temperature water

1 lemon, juiced

1 T raw apple cider vinegar *

**1 tsp raw honey, maple syrup,
or a few drops stevia to taste** (optional)

Dash sea salt

_____

Mix and enjoy!

* If you feel nauseous or experience tightness in the chest after drinking the morning tonic, omit the raw apple cider vinegar.

This reaction can occur when the body releases bacteria and toxins during detox. Continue to drink the Lemon Cravings Blaster without the apple cider vinegar.

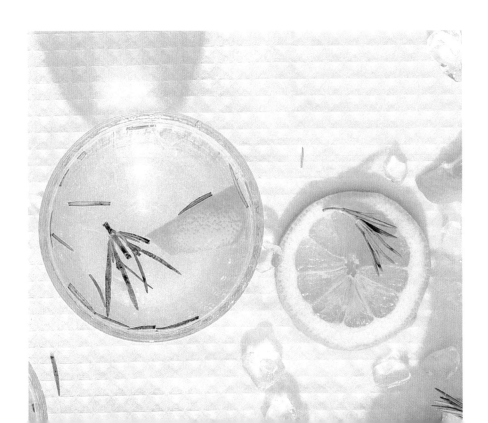

CRANBERRY FLUSH

2 MIN · MAKES 1

2 T cranberry juice concentrate *

1 tsp Psyllium powder

12 oz. water

Juice from 1 lemon

Dash of cinnamon

1 teaspoon of raw honey, maple syrup, or stevia to taste (optional)

Mix and enjoy!

* If you cannot find cranberry juice concentrate, you can use pomegranate or cherry concentrate instead.

2 / SMOOTHIES

PUMPKIN
SMOOTHIE

2 MIN · MAKES 1

1 ½ cups dairy free milk or water

¼ can pumpkin puree
BPA-free can

½ avocado

4 kale leaves

1 tsp vanilla extract

½ tsp no-sugar pumpkin spice

Blend and enjoy!

GREEN MAGIC
SMOOTHIE

2 MIN · MAKES 1

1 ½ cups dairy free milk or water

2 cups spinach

½ avocado

½ tsp cinnamon

1 tsp coconut oil

1 tsp raw cacao powder

Blend and enjoy!

Sweeteners
You may choose
to sweeten any of
the smoothie recipes
with stevia.

SMOOTHIES

CHOCOLATE-COVERED
BLUEBERRY SMOOTHIE

1 2 MIN · MAKES 1

½ cup dairy-free milk
unsweetened

2 cups spinach

½ cup frozen blueberries

1 ¼ cups berries

1 scoop chocolate protein powder

Blend and enjoy!

CHERRY BLISS
SMOOTHIE

2 MIN · MAKES 1

1 ½ cups dairy free milk or water

½ cup fresh or frozen cherries

½ avocado

1 cup spinach

2 T raw cacao powder

1 T coconut oil

Dash of cayenne

Blend and enjoy!

EASY GREEN SMOOTHIE

2 MIN · MAKES 1

1 ½ cups dairy-free milk or water

2 cups spinach

1 green apple

½ avocado

1 T flax seeds

Dash of ginger powder

Blend and enjoy!

DATE SMOOTHIE

2 MIN · MAKES 1

1 ½ cups dairy-free milk or water

4 kale leaves

1 date without pit

¼ tsp alcohol-free vanilla extract

1 T flax meal

Dash of cinnamon

Blend and enjoy!

SUGAR KNOCKOUT

WELLNESS 101
SMOOTHIE

2 MIN · MAKES 1

1 ½ cups dairy-free milk or water

2 cups spinach

½ avocado

½ orange peeled

1 T flax seeds

Dash of cinnamon

Blend and enjoy!

3 / BREAKFAST

CHIA PUDDING

5 MIN · MAKES 1

1 cup dairy-free milk

⅓ cup chia seeds

Fresh, in-season fruit, chopped
apple, orange, grapefruit, pear, etc.

———————————

Add dairy-free milk and chia seeds
to a bowl.

Mix and let it sit for about
5 minutes so the chia seeds can
absorb the milk.

Top with fresh, in-season fruit.

To make warm pudding,
simply heat the milk in
a saucepan over medium
heat for 2–3 minutes. Be
sure to not boil the milk.

Add the milk to the
chia seeds, mix and top
with fresh fruit.

OVERNIGHT OATS
BERRY JAR

5 MIN + 8 HRS · MAKES 1

½ cup gluten-free oats

½ cup unsweetened almond milk

¾ cup frozen berries

Add the oats to a jar along with the milk and berries.

Stir to combine.

Cover and place in the refrigerator overnight or for at least 8 hours.

VANILLA ALMOND OVERNIGHT QUINOA

5 MIN · MAKES 1

1 cup almond milk

½ cup cooked quinoa

½ cup almond pulp
or almond flour or finely
ground almonds

4 T chia seeds

2 T maple syrup

¼ tsp almond extract

¼ tsp vanilla extract

Stevia, to taste (optional)

Chopped almonds
to garnish (optional)

Divide all ingredients between two mason jars.

Stir until incorporated.

Place in refrigerator and let sit overnight.

Remove and garnish with chopped almonds. Enjoy!

EASY PUMPKIN PANCAKES

25 MIN · MAKES 3

½ cup egg whites
about 4 eggs

½ cup pure pumpkin

1 scoop vanilla protein powder

Cinnamon, to taste

Blend together and cook on
a skillet.

PEANUT BUTTER
BANANA WAFFLES

25 MIN · MAKES 3

½ cup gluten-free flour

1 ½ tsp coconut sugar

½ tsp baking powder

½ tsp sea salt

1 egg

1 cup dairy-free milk

4 T coconut oil melted and divided

1 ½ bananas sliced

¼ cup peanut butter

No waffle maker?
Make as pancakes instead.

In a medium bowl, whisk together flour, sugar, baking powder and salt.

Add in egg, milk, and 3 tablespoons of oil. Whisk until smooth and set aside.

Coat the waffle maker* with a small amount of remaining oil.

Add the batter to cover the maker, no more than ⅓ cup at a time.

Cook the waffles about 4 minutes or until golden brown.

Repeat the process until all batter is cooked.

Top with banana and peanut butter before serving. Enjoy!

SATURDAY MORNING
POWER SKILLET

15 MIN · MAKES 2

2 strips nitrate-free bacon

2 T olive oil

1 sweet potato
peeled & cubed in ¼" pieces

¼ red onion diced in ½" pieces

1 clove garlic minced

¼ tsp ground cumin

Pink salt, to taste

Pepper, to taste

4 eggs two eggs per serving

In a sauté pan over medium-high heat, add bacon and olive oil.

When the bacon begins to sizzle, add sweet potatoes and spread out as much as possible to allow the potatoes to rest in the pan in 1 layer. Cook for about 5 minutes or until potatoes start to brown.

Toss potatoes until all sides of potatoes are browned and bacon is crisp (about 3–5 minutes).

While potatoes are cooking, in a separate pan, cook 2–4 eggs to your liking.

Add onions, garlic, and cumin, then season with salt and pepper, allowing everything to sit in the heat of the pan for a minute or two.

Once the eggs are done, add them over the top of the skillet or serve them on the side. Enjoy!

PROSCIUTTO-WRAPPED MINI MUFFINS

25 MIN · MAKES 6

4 T coconut oil

½ medium onion finely diced

3 cloves of garlic minced

½ lb cremini mushrooms thinly sliced

½ lb frozen spinach thawed and squeezed dry

8 large eggs

¼ cup coconut milk

2 T coconut flour

1 cup cherry tomatoes halved

5 oz Prosciutto di Parma

½ tsp Himalayan pink salt

½ tsp black pepper

12-cup muffin tin

Preheat oven to 375°F.

Heat coconut oil over medium heat in a large cast iron skillet. Sauté onion until soft and translucent.

Add garlic and mushrooms and cook until the moisture evaporates.

Season with salt and pepper and spoon to a plate to cool to room temperature.

In a large bowl, beat the eggs with coconut milk, coconut flour, salt, and pepper until combined.

Add the sautéed mushrooms and spinach. Stir to combine.

Brush the remainder of melted coconut oil (from the pan) onto a muffin tin

Line each cup with prosciutto, covering the bottom and sides.

Spoon the egg mixture into the prosciutto cups and top with halved cherry tomatoes.

Bake for 20 minutes, rotating the tray halfway through baking.

Let muffins cool in the pan for a few minutes. Enjoy!!

SCRAMBLED EGGS
WITH TOMATO & AVOCADO

10 MIN · MAKES 1

2 eggs

1 T coconut oil

Sea salt & black pepper
to taste

1 small tomato sliced

½ avocado sliced

Crack the eggs into a small bowl

Using a fork or whisk, beat the eggs until the yolks and egg whites are uniform.

Set the eggs to the side.

Place a pan over medium heat and add coconut oil.

When the coconut oil is melted, add the eggs.

Use a rubber spatula to fold the eggs towards the center until you no longer see any liquid (about three minutes).

Season with salt and pepper as you fold.

When the eggs are done, serve on a plate with sliced tomato and avocado.

TURKEY SAUSAGE SCRAMBLE

10 MIN · MAKES 1

4 turkey sausage links
casing removed

1/4 cup spinach

2 eggs, whisked

Sea salt & black pepper
to taste

Heat a pan over medium heat then add the sausage to the pan.

Brown for five to six minutes or until cooked through, breaking it up as it cooks.

Add the spinach to the pan and move it around until it's wilted.

Move the sausage and spinach to one side of the pan and pour the eggs into the empty side.

Stir the eggs frequently as they cook. Incorporate the spinach and sausage into the egg once the eggs are cooked through.

Season with salt and pepper if needed and enjoy!

4 / SOUPS

SMOKY LIME AVOCADO SOUP

15 MIN · MAKES 2

2 avocados

1 bunch cilantro roughly chopped

1 celery stalk roughly chopped

1 garlic clove minced

1 tsp cumin

½ tsp smoked paprika

1 lime juiced

1 cup water

Sea salt & black pepper to taste

This is a raw soup.

Add all the ingredients to a blender. Blend until smooth and serve immediately.

CREAMY SPINACH SOUP

15 MIN · MAKES 2

½ **bunch spinach** roughly chopped

1 **avocado** roughly chopped

1 **cucumber** roughly chopped

1 **garlic clove** chopped

1 **cup water**

1 **lemon** juiced

Sea salt & black pepper to taste

This is a raw soup.

Blend all the ingredients together until smooth and serve in a bowl.

CHICKEN
MINESTRONE SOUP

30 MIN · MAKES 4-6

2 T coconut oil

1 onion chopped

1 carrot chopped

2 celery stalks chopped

2 garlic cloves chopped

2 zucchinis chopped

Sea salt & black pepper to taste

2 T Italian seasoning

15-oz can cannellini beans

28-oz can diced tomatoes

32-oz box vegetable broth

2 cups boneless chicken breast *
chopped

Heat the oil in a large soup pot.

Add the onion, carrot, celery, garlic, zucchini, sea salt, black pepper and Italian seasoning.

Sauté until the vegetables are soft.

Next, add the beans, tomatoes, vegetable broth, and chopped chicken.

Cover and let the pot simmer for about 20 minutes. Serve hot.

* **Where do you find chopped chicken breast?** You can buy a whole, roasted chicken from your favorite grocery store. Remove the chicken breasts and chop them into bite-sized pieces.

CHICKEN TORTILLA SOUP

45 MIN · MAKES 4

2 T coconut oil

2 boneless chicken breasts

Sea salt & black pepper to taste

1 onion chopped

1 jalapeño (optional)

2 garlic cloves chopped

1 cup frozen corn

32-oz box of chicken or vegetable broth

15.5-oz can of black beans rinsed

14.5-oz can diced tomatoes

1 T cumin

1 bunch fresh cilantro chopped

2 handfuls of organic corn chips crumbled

Add coconut oil to a large soup pot over medium heat.

Add the chicken breasts with sea salt & black pepper.

Cook on both sides until it is no longer pink in the middle. Remove the chicken from the pot and set to the side.

Next, add the onion, jalapeño, garlic, corn, broth, black beans, tomatoes, and cumin to the large soup pot.

Mix well until simmering.

Chop up the cooked chicken and add to the pot.

Add the cilantro and turn off the flame. Let the pot sit for about 30 minutes before serving.

Serve hot in a bowl topped with crumbled corn chips.

BLACK BEAN SOUP

30 MIN · MAKES 4-6

2 T coconut oil

2 celery stalks chopped

1 onion chopped

1 green bell pepper chopped

3 garlic cloves chopped

1 T cumin

1 bay leaf

3 15-oz cans of black beans drained and rinsed

32-oz box of vegetable broth

1 bunch cilantro chopped

1 avocado sliced

Heat the oil in a large soup pot.

Add the celery, onion, bell pepper, garlic, cumin and bay leaf.

Sauté until the vegetables are soft. Add the black beans and broth.

Cover and cook for about 20 min. Use the back of a spoon to mash the beans while you stir to make a thicker soup consistency.

Add the chopped cilantro to the pot during the last 5 minutes.

Serve with sliced avocado.

ROASTED GARLIC
SOUP WITH SHRIMP

30 MIN · MAKES 4-6

2 garlic bulbs cloves removed

1 onion, chopped

1 T rosemary

1 tsp turmeric

Sea salt & black pepper
o taste

2 T coconut oil melted

32-oz box vegetable broth

1 lb shrimp (optional)
fresh or frozen
peeled and deveined

Sea salt & black pepper to taste

Preheat the oven to 400° F.

Add the garlic, onion, rosemary, turmeric, sea salt and black pepper to a large bowl.

Add melted coconut oil; mix well.

Layer onto a roasting pan and bake for about 20–25 minutes. Vegetables should be soft and brown when done.

Remove vegetables from pan and place in a blender.

Add the vegetable broth and blend until smooth.

Place the mix in a large soup bowl and bring to a boil.

Turn down the heat to low and add the shrimp. Shrimp are done when opaque (about 3–5 minutes*).

Serve the soup hot.

* DO NOT let the shrimp overcook as it will have a rubbery texture.

CREAM OF MUSHROOM SOUP WITH SHREDDED CHICKEN

30 MIN · MAKES 4–6

2 T coconut oil

1 onion chopped

6 cups mushrooms
(use a mix of your favorite)

3 garlic cloves

1 tsp thyme

13.5-oz can coconut milk

½ cup vegetable broth

Sea salt & black pepper to taste

4 cups spinach

2 cups shredded chicken*
(optional)

Add the coconut oil, onion, mushrooms, garlic and thyme to a large soup pot.

Sauté for about 5 minutes to allow the vegetables to become soft.

Add coconut milk, vegetable broth, sea salt and black pepper.

Cover and bring to a boil.

Turn down the flame and add the spinach. Let it simmer for about 5 minutes.

Feel free to use an immersion blender or high-speed blender to make the soup smooth.

Top with chicken and serve.

* Where do you find chopped chicken breast?

You can buy a whole, roasted chicken from your favorite grocery store. Remove the chicken breasts and chop them into bite-sized pieces.

5 / SALADS

SALMON SALAD WITH FRESH GREENS

10 MIN · MAKES 2

6-oz can of wild salmon
or freshly cooked

4 cups mixed greens

1 tsp dried dill

1 large cucumber chopped

1 cup shredded carrot

1 cup grape tomatoes

¼ cup black olives stored in water

Remove salmon from the can and drain the water.

Place it into a bowl and use your fork to mash the salmon into smaller pieces. Set it to the side.

Add the remaining salad ingredients to a large bowl.

Top with your salmon and your favorite dressing.

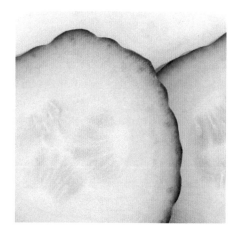

SIGNATURE STEAK SALAD

20 MIN · MAKES 4

1 lbs skirt steak
trimmed of excess fat, halved
crosswise (at room temperature)

1–2 T extra virgin olive oil

2 cups cherry tomatoes halved

½ lb baby arugula
or lettuce of choice

½ cup roasted peppers

½ sliced avocado

Choice of dressing
suggested: balsamic

CAST-IRON SKILLET
Heat skillet on medium-high to high and
add olive oil.

When oil begins to simmer, place steak in
skillet and do not move for 5 minutes.

Turn it once, and cook for another
3 minutes to medium-rare (or more or less
depending on preference).

ON A GRILL
Prepare grill for direct-heat cooking over
hot charcoal or high heat for gas.

Oil grill rack, then grill steak, covered only
if using a gas grill, turning once, 4–6 minutes total for medium-rare.

———————————

Transfer steak to a cutting board and let rest,
loosely covered with foil, for 5 min.

Arrange arugula on a platter.

Thinly slice steak on the diagonal, across
the grain. Arrange over arugula, then toss
remaining ingredients on top.

Drizzle dressing on top and serve.

TACO SALAD
IN A JAR

20 MIN · MAKES 4

1 lb ground meat
beef, chicken, turkey, etc.

2 cups salsa organic store-bought
brands are fine

2 cups carrots shredded

2–3 tomatoes chopped

2 heads of romaine lettuce chopped

1 avocado chopped

2 cups organic corn chips

4 wide-mouth mason jars
16-oz

Cook your ground meat in a pan over medium heat. Use a spatula or fork to break it up into crumbled pieces.

The meat is done when it is browned all the way through.

Be sure to drain as much of the excess oil as possible.

Add the following ingredients to each jar in the following order:

· ½ cup of salsa
· ½ cup of meat
· shredded carrots
· tomatoes
· chopped romaine
· avocado

Crumble corn chips on top of the avocado and cover with the lid.

Store in the refrigerator until you are ready to eat.

TUNA SALAD

10 MIN · MAKES 2

6-oz can of tuna
drained of excess liquid

2 apples chopped

½ cup walnuts chopped

1 cucumber chopped

1 cup shredded carrots

1 lemon juiced

1 tsp dried basil

Sea salt & black pepper to taste

2 T extra virgin olive oil

Empty the can of drained tuna into a large mixing bowl. Use a fork to mash it into small pieces.

Add the remaining ingredients and mix well.

CHICKPEA SALAD

10 MIN · MAKES 2

1 cup cooked chickpeas canned is fine (drained and rinsed)

4 cups romaine lettuce chopped

½ cup carrot shredded

1 celery stalk chopped

½ cup black olives canned in water

Handful of grape tomatoes halved

Sea salt & black pepper to taste

Add the ingredients to a large bowl and top with your favorite salad dressing.

SIMPLE GREEK
SALAD

10 MIN · MAKES 2

2–3 cups romaine lettuce chopped

½ tomato chopped

½ cucumber sliced

2 T red onion chopped

¼ cup Kalamata olives (optional)

¼ cup pepperoncini (optional)

2 T Greek dressing

Protein of choice
Chicken suggested

Combine all ingredients in a bowl and toss.

Top with your protein of choice and enjoy!

PEACH
CAPRESE SALAD

5 MIN · MAKES 1

2 medium tomatoes sliced

1 peach peeled and sliced

¼ cup fresh basil

¼ cup mozzarella pearls

1 T olive oil

Balsamic glaze (pre-made is fine)

Sea salt & black pepper to taste

Alternate slices of tomato, peach, and basil.

Sprinkle mozzarella on top or in the middle.

Drizzle with olive oil. Sprinkle with salt and pepper to taste.

Finish by drizzling balsamic glaze on top. Enjoy!

APPLE WALNUT
SALAD

10 MIN · MAKES 2

4 cups mixed greens

1 apple chopped

½ cup walnuts chopped

1 cucumber chopped

½ cup grated carrot

½ cup sprouts

—————————

Add the ingredients to a bowl
and mix well.

Top with creamy avocado dressing
(found in Dressings chapter).

6 / CHICKEN TURKEY BEEF

SLOW COOKER CHICKEN CACCIATORE

6 HRS · MAKES 4-6

6–8 chicken thighs boneless skinless

1 medium onion chopped

4 garlic cloves minced

1½ T balsamic vinegar

1 T olive oil

28-oz crushed tomatoes

8 oz mushrooms sliced

2 tsp Italian seasoning

¼ cup olives (optional)

Sea salt & black pepper to taste

Season chicken with salt and pepper.

Heat olive oil in a pan and sear chicken on both sides to brown. Add to slow cooker.

Cook onion in the pan you just seared the chicken in for about 3 minutes.

Add garlic and 1 T balsamic.

Cook for 1 more minute and add to slow cooker.

Top chicken with tomatoes, mushrooms, and Italian seasoning.

Cook on low for 6 hours or on high for 2–3 hours.

Add ½ T of balsamic to slow cooker just before serving.

GO-TO CHICKEN
SALAD ROLL UPS

10 MIN · MAKES 1

4–8 oz chicken breast
precooked and chopped

2–3 butter lettuce leaves

¼ cup almonds chopped

¼ cup red seedless grapes halved

¼ avocado mashed

Sea salt & black pepper to taste

─────────────

Mix all ingredients (minus the
lettuce leaves) in a bowl.

Spoon into butter lettuce leaves
to make a nice wrap!

GINGER CHICKEN WITH SAUTEED VEGETABLES

40 MIN + MARINATING · MAKES 2

2 chicken breasts sliced

1 T coconut oil

1 inch piece of fresh ginger grated

1 lime juiced

1 tsp garlic powder

Sea salt & black pepper to taste

1 onion chopped

1 small purple cabbage chopped

1 cup shredded carrots

Place sliced chicken, coconut oil, ginger, lime juice, garlic, sea salt, and black pepper to a large plastic bag.

Mix the ingredients well and close the bag. Place in the refrigerator and marinate for a minimum of 30 minutes (overnight is best).

When you are ready to cook the chicken, add about a tablespoon of coconut oil to a hot pan.

Add the contents of the plastic bag to the pan and sauté until chicken is cooked all the way through. Remove from pan and set it to the side.

Add the onion, purple cabbage and carrots to the pan. Sauté well. Add a touch of salt and pepper if needed.

When the vegetables are wilted to your liking, serve with the chicken.

CHICKEN, TURKEY, BEEF

CHICKEN FAJITAS

25 MIN · MAKES 2

2 T coconut oil

2 chicken breasts

1 tsp cumin

1 tsp chili powder

Sea salt & black pepper to taste

**4–6 brown rice tortillas
or coconut flour wraps**

1 head romaine lettuce chopped

1 cup guacamole

Add coconut oil to a hot pan. When the oil is melted, add the chicken breasts.

Quickly season the chicken with cumin, chili powder, sea salt, and black pepper.

Cook on both sides until the chicken is no longer pink on the inside.

Once the chicken is done, set it to the side for about 10 minutes.

Slice the chicken and place on a warm tortilla. Top with lettuce and guacamole.

CHICKEN, TURKEY, BEEF

SESAME-CRUSTED TURKEY

30 MIN · MAKES 3-4

1 lb organic turkey loin

1 ½ oz toasted sesame seeds

1 tsp ground cumin

1 tsp lemon pepper

1 egg white lightly beaten

1 pinch salt

1 T extra virgin olive oil

Preheat oven to 400°F.

Mix the sesame seeds, cumin, and lemon pepper together in a large bowl.

Preheat a sauté pan to medium-high.

Season the turkey with ¼ tsp salt.

Dip the turkey in the egg, allowing the excess to drip off, then coat it completely with sesame seeds.

Add 1 tablespoon olive oil to the sauté pan and sear crusted turkey for 1-2 minutes on each side until crispy and golden, then place in a glass baking dish.

Roast in oven for 15 minutes or until internal temperature reaches 150°F.

Let rest 5 minutes.

HUMMUS CHICKEN

40 MIN · MAKES 3

3 chicken breasts boneless, skinless

1 yellow squash sliced

1 zucchini sliced

1 red bell pepper chopped

1 medium onion chopped

2 lemons

Sea salt & black pepper to taste

Italian seasoning

½ cup hummus
homemade or store-bought

2 T dried rosemary

1 T extra virgin olive oil

1 tsp smoked paprika

Generous drizzle of balsamic vinegar

Preheat oven to 450°F. Lightly coat one large baking dish with 1 tbsp olive oil.

Season the chicken breasts with salt, pepper, and Italian seasoning.

In a large bowl, toss the sliced zucchini, squash and onion with 1 tbsp olive oil until evenly coated.

Season with salt, pepper, and Italian seasoning.

Cover each chicken breast with ¼ cup of hummus each.

Place all vegetables in an even layer on the bottom of a 9×13 dish. Lay the chicken evenly on top.

Squeeze the juice of one lemon over the chicken and vegetables.

Lightly season the entire dish with chopped rosemary and paprika.

Thinly slice the remaining lemon, and place a few slices in the dish.

Drizzle balsamic vinegar over the top, and bake for 25–30 minutes, or until the chicken is cooked through and the vegetables are tender. Serve immediately.

CHICKEN, TURKEY, BEEF

CHICKEN WITH SAUTÉED ONION & LEMON

40 MIN · MAKES 3

6 chicken thighs bone-in, with skin

1 T coconut oil

1 sweet onion
halved and thinly sliced

1–2 garlic cloves thinly sliced

½ lemon thinly sliced

¼ cup chicken or vegetable broth
organic

2 T fresh flat leaf parsley

Sea salt & black pepper to taste

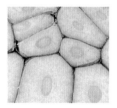

Season chicken with salt and pepper.

Heat coconut oil in a large sauté pan over medium heat, and place chicken skin-side down.

Turn chicken over when the skin is well browned.

When both sides are browned and cooked through, remove chicken from pan and continue with remaining pieces. Remove chicken from pan. Pour off all but 2 T's of the remaining oil. Add onions. Season with salt and pepper, to taste. Sauté onions until almost golden brown. Add the garlic and cook until onions are golden.

Add the lemon slices and sauté for 1 min.

Add the stock and stir.

Add the chicken back to the pan.

Add the parsley and stir.

Check for proper seasoning. Enjoy!

CILANTRO LIME CHICKEN

40 MIN · MAKES 3-4

1 lb chicken breasts organic

1 T extra virgin olive oil

1 lime juice and zest

2 T fresh cilantro coarsely chopped

½ jalapeño coarsely chopped (optional)

1 clove garlic coarsely chopped

Sea salt & black pepper to taste

Preheated oven or grill to 400° F.

Puree the oil, lime, juice and zest, cilantro, jalapeno, and garlic in a food processor until smooth.

Place the chicken on a foil-lined baking sheet, pat dry, and season with salt and pepper.

Cover the chicken with the cilantro-lime mixture and bake (or grill) until internal temperature reaches 165° (about 25–35 minutes).

CHIMICHURRI STEAK

40 MIN · MAKES 3–4

CHIMICHURRI SAUCE

1 cup flat-leaf parsley fresh

¼ cup fresh cilantro

½ cup extra virgin olive oil

⅓ cup red wine vinegar

2 cloves garlic

½ tsp cumin powder

½ tsp red pepper flakes

½ tsp sea salt

2 boneless ribeye steaks 8 oz each

1 T balsamic vinegar

Extra virgin olive oil

Sea salt & black pepper to taste

Let steaks sit out for about 30 minutes to bring to room temperature.

While steaks are tempering, blend all chimichurri sauce ingredients in a food processor until smooth.

Season steaks with salt and pepper, then drizzle with balsamic vinegar and just enough olive oil to coat.

Heat a grill pan over medium heat. Add steaks and cook for 4–5 minutes, then flip and cook an additional 5–6 minutes. Do not move the steaks while cooking.

Remove from pan and let rest about 5 minutes.

Slice the meat into thin strips and drizzle with the chimichurri sauce.

Serve and enjoy!

EASY GRASS-FED BEEF BURGERS

40 MIN · MAKES 3

1 lb ground beef grass-fed

Himalayan pink salt

Black pepper fresh ground

Any other seasoning you like!

Take meat out of the fridge and allow it to come to room temperature (20–30 minutes).

Divide the meat into three parts and, by hand, form patties.

Heat a sauté pan to medium heat.

Season both sides of the patties with salt and pepper (and any other seasoning you like).

Place all 3 patties in the pan and sear for 3–5 minutes on each side.

Remove from pan and allow to rest for a few minutes before serving.

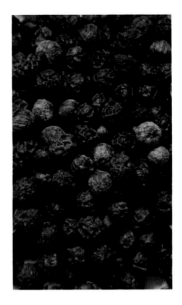

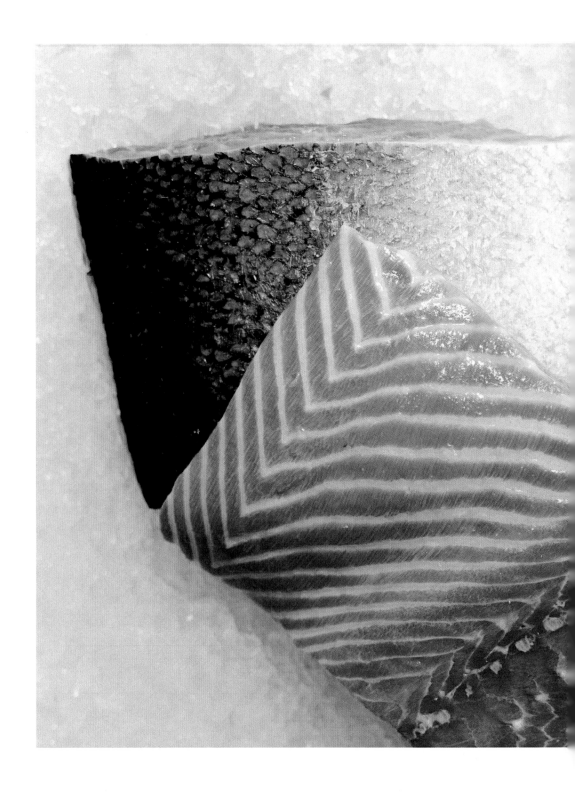

7 / FISH & SEAFOOD

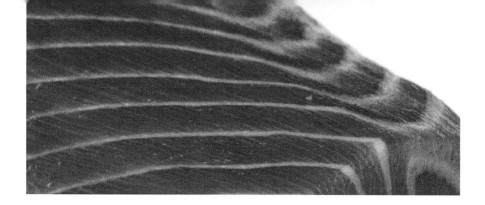

GRILLED SALMON KEBABS

20 MIN · MAKES 4

1 ½ tsp parsley

2 tsp sesame seeds

½ tsp sea salt

⅛ tsp black pepper

Pinch red pepper flakes optional

3 T maple syrup

1 T extra virgin olive oil

2 salmon filets cut into 1" cubes

2 lemons sliced

Skewers

Preheat grill to medium.

In a mixing bowl, combine parsley, sesame seeds, sea salt, black pepper, red pepper flakes, maple syrup and olive oil. Mix well.

Add the salmon pieces and toss to coat.

Take your skewers and slide on a piece of salmon, followed by a folded lemon slice. Repeat until all ingredients are used up.

Grill kebabs for about 3–4 minutes per side, or until salmon flakes with a fork.

Remove from the grill and divide between plates. Enjoy!

SAUTÉED KALE
WITH SHRIMP

15 MIN · MAKES 2

2 T coconut oil

1 onion chopped

1 garlic clove chopped

1 bunch kale

Sea salt & black pepper to taste

1 lb of shrimp
fresh or frozen, devined

Add about half the coconut oil to a hot pan with onion and garlic. Sauté for about 5 minutes until fragrant.

Add kale and cook until wilted.

Season with sea salt and pepper, then remove from pan and set aside.

Add remaining coconut oil to the same pan and let it melt.

Add the shrimp along with a pinch of sea salt and black pepper to taste.

Sauté the shrimp for 2–5 minutes, until the shrimp is opaque in color.

Serve with the kale.

CAULIFLOWER MASH WITH BAKED SALMON

25 MIN · MAKES 2

4 salmon steaks or filets

2 T coconut oil

1 large head of cauliflower chopped

1 tsp thyme

1 tsp garlic powder

¼ cup dairy-free milk unsweetened

Sea salt & black pepper to taste

2 chives chopped

2 scallions chopped

1 tsp sesame seeds

Preheat oven to 450° F.

Coat salmon with coconut oil and place on a roasting pan. Sprinkle with sea salt and black pepper

Bake 12–15 minutes until the salmon is cooked all the way through.

Add about one inch of water to a large pot with a metal steam basket and place on high heat.

Add chopped cauliflower. Cover and steam the cauliflower for 5–7 minutes until soft.

Remove from the steamer and place in a blender or food processor with thyme, garlic, milk, salt, and pepper.

Serve warm with baked salmon.

Top the dish with chives, scallions, and sesame seeds.

PAN-SEARED TOMATO BASIL TROUT

15 MIN · MAKES 2

1 oz pancetta chopped

1 cup cherry tomatoes halved

½ tsp garlic minced

½ tsp black pepper freshly ground, divided

¼ tsp Himalayan salt divided

¼ cup small basil leaves

1 T olive oil divided

2 trout fillets 12-16 oz total

2 lemon wedges

Over low heat, heat pancetta in skillet. Cook just until pancetta begins to brown (about 4 minutes).

Add cherry tomatoes, garlic, and half of the pepper and salt.

Cook for 3 minutes or until tomatoes begin to soften.

Remove from the heat and stir in basil leaves.

Heat another large, non-stick skillet to medium-high. Add enough oil to lightly coat the bottom of the pan.

Sprinkle fish evenly with remaining salt and pepper and add to pan.

Cook for 2 minutes on each side or until fish flakes with a fork.

Remove fish from pan and top with tomato sauté.

Serve with lemon wedges.

CITRUS FISH TACOS

10 MIN + MARINATING· MAKES 2

2 tilapia fillets
wild-caught, cut in 1" chunks

MARINADE

2 large oranges juiced

½ lime juiced

3 T olive oil

1 tsp cumin

½ tsp sea salt

4–6 gluten-free wraps

½ red pepper diced

¼ red onion diced

½ mango diced

½ avocado sliced

Mix the orange juice, lime juice, olive oil, cumin, and salt in a bowl and combine well.

Gently place the pieces of tilapia into a large Ziploc bag and pour in the marinade.

Marinate for 2–4 hours in the refrigerator, flipping the bag over about halfway through.

Heat some olive or coconut oil in a large skillet. When the pan is warm, add the marinated tilapia and cook for 8-9 minutes, flipping only once.

Prepare the tacos to your liking, adding fish, pepper, onion, and mango.

Be creative and add anything else you think may taste great on there!

LEMON BUTTER HALIBUT

20 MIN · MAKES 4

4 firm white halibut filets
Substitute: cod or mahi

3 T grass-fed butter melted

1 lemon juice and zest

1 tsp sea salt

1 tsp paprika

1 tsp garlic powder

1 tsp onion powder

⅛ tsp black pepper

3 T olive oil

Lemon slices for serving, optional

Pat-dry fish filets and set aside.

Combine melted butter, lemon juice and zest, and ½ tsp salt.

In a separate bowl, combine the remaining salt with the paprika, garlic powder, onion powder, and black pepper.

Evenly press spice mixture onto all sides of fish.

Heat olive oil in a large, heavy pan over medium-high heat.

Once oil is sizzling, add filets and cook each side about 2–3 minutes.

While cooking, lightly drizzle some of the lemon butter sauce, reserving the rest for serving.

When fish is browned and somewhat firm in the center, remove from heat.

Season with extra salt & pepper to taste.

CHIPOTLE SALMON BURGER WITH MANGO SALSA

20 MIN · MAKES 3

1 lb salmon
wild-caught, if possible

2 T chipotle peppers in adobo sauce
chopped

1 T + 1 tsp wholegrain mustard

1 lime zested

½ lime juiced

½ tsp salt

¼ tsp pepper

1 T extra virgin olive oil

Mango salsa (p. 159) to serve

Combine all ingredients (except oil and mango salsa) in a food processor and pulse for 30 seconds.

If no food processor is available, finely dice the salmon and combine all ingredients in a large mixing bowl.

Divide mixture into 3 burger patties.

Preheat skillet on medium for 1 minute.

Drizzle olive oil and sear burgers for 3–4 minutes on each side until golden brown.

GRILLED LIME-BASIL
TUNA STEAKS

20 MIN · MAKES 2

2 tuna steaks

MARINADE

1 T olive oil plus more to drizzle

1 lime juiced

1 T basil leaves chopped

1 garlic clove minced

⅓ tsp pepper

1 tsp sea salt

1 large tomato chopped

1 cucumber chopped

½ lemon juiced

Olive oil

Sea salt & black pepper to taste

Basil leaves for garnish

In a small bowl, combine the olive oil, lime juice, basil, garlic, salt and pepper. Mix well.

Add the tuna steaks to a Ziploc bag and pour in the marinade. Shake well then place in the refridgerator while you prep the rest.

Combine the diced tomato and cucumber together in a bowl. Drizzle with a bit of olive oil and lemon juice, then season with sea salt and black pepper to taste. Set aside.

Preheat the grill to medium.

Grill the marinated steaks for about 4 minutes per side, or until they are cooked to your liking.

Remove fish from the grill and plate on a bed of the cucumber-tomato salad and garnish with basil.

8 / VEGETARIAN

CREAMY PASTA
WITH KALE

40 MIN · MAKES 3

1 cup chickpea pasta

2 cups kale chopped

¼ cup sun-dried tomatoes chopped (optional)

2 garlic cloves minced

⅔ cup cashews soaked for 30 min. and drained

½ cup water

½ tsp nutritional yeast (optional)

1 T lemon juice

2 T olive oil

Sea salt & black pepper to taste

Cook the pasta according to the directions on the package and set aside.

Heat a pan over medium-low heat.

Sauté the kale, sun-dried tomatoes, and garlic for 5–7 minutes.

Mix in the cooked pasta and turn off the heat.

Add the remaining ingredients to a food processor and blend on high until smooth.

Toss the pasta with the cream sauce and enjoy!

TOFU VEGGIE FRIED RICE

35 MIN · MAKES 4

¾ cup jasmine rice uncooked

½ T sesame oil

1 package extra firm tofu (drained and diced)

Sea salt & black pepper to taste

1 head of broccoli chopped

½ head purple cabbage thinly sliced

1 medium carrot diced

4 eggs whisked

4 T tamari or coconut aminos

3 green onions sliced

Cook the jasmine rice according to package directions.

Heat half of the sesame oil in a large non-stick pan over medium heat

Cook the tofu for about 5 minutes or until browned, frequently tossing.

Season with salt and pepper and transfer to a bowl.

In the same pan, heat the remaining sesame oil over medium heat.

Stir fry the broccoli, purple cabbage, and carrots until fork-tender, 5–7 minutes.

Slide the veggies to the side of the pan and add the eggs.

Gently push the eggs back and forth with your spatula until scrambled and cooked through.

Add the rice over top of the eggs and break it up with your spatula.

Add the tofu and tamari. Gently stir until everything is well combined.

Divide into bowls, garnish with green onions, and enjoy!

GRILLED PORTOBELLO BURGERS WITH GOAT CHEESE

25 MIN · MAKES 2

½ cup red onion sliced

1 zucchini sliced into rounds

1 yellow pepper sliced into strips

1 T olive oil

Sea salt & black pepper to taste

4 portobello mushroom caps

1 ½ cups lentils cooked

⅓ cup goat cheese

Mixed greens

Preheat grill to medium-high heat.

In a mixing bowl, combine red onion, zucchini, and yellow pepper. Drizzle with olive oil and season with sea salt and black pepper to taste. Toss well.

Transfer to a grilling basket and place on the grill. Grill for 15 minutes, or until slightly charred. Toss periodically.

Brush the insides of the portobello mushroom caps with olive oil and place face down on the grill. Cook for about 5 minutes, flipping halfway.

Remove grilled veggies and mushrooms from the grill, then fill two mushroom caps with the grilled veggies. Top with lentils and mixed greens.

Fill the other two portobello caps with goat cheese and place it on top to form a burger.

Serve any leftover veggies as a salad on the side. Enjoy!

MEXICAN
QUINOA WRAPS

45 MIN · MAKES 8

½ cup water

2 cups black beans cooked

3 cups tomatoes diced
canned or fresh

1 cup corn fresh or frozen

1½ tsp cumin

½ tsp paprika

2 T chili powder

2 tsp sea salt

¾ cup quinoa dry, uncooked

8 whole wheat tortillas

1 cup fresh spinach

2 avocados diced

In a large pot over medium heat, add water, black beans, tomatoes, corn, cumin, paprika, chili powder, and salt. Bring to a simmer.

Add quinoa and cook for 12–15 more minutes.

Place tortillas on a plate and top with spinach, avocado, and the quinoa filling. Enjoy!

SOUTHWEST
TOFU BURRITO

20 MIN · MAKES 4

2 T coconut oil

1 large onion chopped

2 garlic cloves chopped

1 large red bell pepper chopped

1 large green bell pepper chopped

2 large tomatoes chopped

2 packages extra firm tofu drained

1 T turmeric powder

1 T taco or fajita seasoning salt-free

Sea salt & black pepper to taste

1 bunch cilantro chopped

4 large collard leaves
bottom stem removed

1 cup salsa

2 avocados sliced

Add coconut oil to a large skillet over medium heat and add onion, garlic, bell peppers, and tomato.

Sauté for about 5 minutes.

Break tofu into bite-sized pieces and season with turmeric powder, taco or fajita seasoning, salt, and pepper. Mix well. The color should be uniform.

Stir in cilantro.

Serve inside a collard leaf and top with salsa and avocado. Roll like a burrito.

WINTER BUDDHA BOWL

40 MIN · MAKES 4

1 head cauliflower cut into florets

1 carrot cut into rounds

1 turnip chopped into 1" pieces

1 parsnip chopped into 1" pieces

1 beet chopped into 1" pieces

DRESSING

¾ cup tahini

2 T extra virgin olive oil

1 lemon juiced

1 clove garlic minced

½ tsp sea salt

3 T warm water

15-oz can chickpeas drained and rinsed

1 cup quinoa cooked

1 bunch kale leaves

Preheat oven to 420° F.

Place cauliflower florets, carrots, beet, turnip, and parsnip in a large mixing bowl.

Season with sea salt and pepper and drizzle with a splash of olive oil. Toss well. Toss beets separately if you want to avoid staining the other veggies.

Bake in oven for 30 minutes.

Prepare dressing by combining tahini, olive oil, lemon juice, minced garlic, and sea salt together in a mason jar. Add warm water and shake well.

If dressing is too thick, add small amounts of water to reach desired consistency.

Place the kale in a bowl and massage with a bit of extra virgin olive oil. Season with sea salt.

Heat a skillet to medium and sauté the kale just until wilted. Transfer to a bowl.

Pour chickpeas into the same frying pan (which should still be lightly oiled) and sauté until slightly browned.

Assemble your Buddha bowls by dividing quinoa between the bowls and arranging roasted vegetables, sautéed kale, and warm chickpeas on the top.

Drizzle desired amount of dressing over the bowl. Enjoy!

VEGETARIAN

PAN-SEARED TOFU WITH SAUTÉED VEGETABLES

30 MIN + MARINATING · MAKES 4

1 package extra-firm tofu cut into ½" slices

MARINADE

¼ cup soy sauce

1" piece of ginger grated

1 T maple syrup

1 tsp apple cider vinegar

1 tsp sesame oil

2 T of coconut oil

1 red bell pepper chopped

1 onion chopped

1 head broccoli chopped

Add the soy sauce, ginger, maple syrup, vinegar, and sesame oil to a large bowl and mix well.

Add the sliced tofu and let it marinate for at least 30 minutes (overnight is best).

Add coconut oil to a skillet and heat to high. Fry the slices of marinated tofu on each side until brown (about 3 minutes). Remove tofu and set aside.

Leaving the pan on high heat, add red bell pepper and onion. Sauté until soft (about 5 minutes).

Add the broccoli and continue sautéing until bright green (about 5 minutes).

RED LENTIL DAAL WITH SPINACH

20 MIN · MAKES 4

1 large onion chopped

2½ cups red lentils washed

5 cups vegetable broth or water

1 garlic clove chopped

2 tsp curry powder

1" piece of ginger grated

1 bunch spinach chopped

1 bunch cilantro chopped

Sea salt & black pepper to taste

Add the onion, lentils, vegetable broth, garlic, curry powder, and ginger to a large pot over high heat.

Once boiling, reduce to a low simmer. Stir every few minutes until the lentils are broken down (10–15 minutes).

Stir in spinach, cilantro, sea salt, and black pepper. Continue to stir until the vegetables are wilted.

9 / SNACKS & SUCH

MAPLE ROASTED ALMONDS

10 MIN · MAKES 4

½ cup almonds

1 ½ tsp maple syrup

½ tsp cinnamon

Place almonds in a frying pan and toast over medium heat. When slightly browned, add maple syrup and cinnamon and stir well. Turn heat back to low. Continuously stir almonds until they become sticky (about 2 minutes).

Remove from heat and spread almonds onto a piece of parchment paper. Let dry for 10 minutes. When cool, break apart and place single portions in snack-sized baggies for an easy grab-and-go snack.

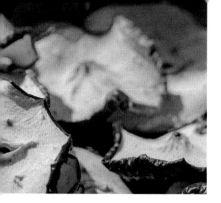

APPLE PIE
PROTEIN BALLS

60 MIN · MAKES 12

1½ cups dried apple
roughly chopped

½ cup coconut flakes
shredded, unsweetened

3 T almond butter

1 tsp cinnamon

½ tsp nutmeg

Add all ingredients to a blender or food processor and blend until well incorporated.

Rub a dab of coconut oil in your hands and roll the mixture into individual balls.

Refrigerate for about an hour before serving.

PUMPKIN
PRUNE BITES

60 MIN · MAKES 12

1 cup pumpkin seeds

¾ cup coconut flakes
shredded, unsweetened

¾ cup rolled oats

½ cup prunes chopped

¼ cup pumpkin puree

1" ginger grated

1 tsp cinnamon

½ tsp nutmeg

Pinch of sea salt

Add all ingredients to a blender or food processor and blend until well incorporated.

Rub a dab of coconut oil in your hands and roll the mixture into individual balls.

Refrigerate for about an hour before serving.

SUPERFOOD ENERGY BALLS

60 MIN · MAKES 12

½ **cup coconut flakes**
shredded, unsweetened

½ **cup rolled oats**

½ **cup almond butter**

¼ **cup hemp seeds**

2 **dates**

1 **T spirulina**

1 **tsp maca powder**

Pinch of sea salt

Add all ingredients to a blender or food processor and blend until well incorporated.

Rub a dab of coconut oil in your hands and roll the mixture into individual balls.

Refrigerate for about an hour before serving.

SNACKS & SUCH

GARLIC-DILL SWEET POTATO CHIPS

30 MIN · MAKES 4

2 large sweet potatoes sliced as thin as possible

2 T coconut oil melted

1 tsp garlic powder

1 tsp dried dill

Sea salt & black pepper to taste

Preheat oven to 450° F.

Combine the melted oil, garlic, dill, sea salt, and black pepper in a large bowl.

Add the sliced sweet potatoes and coat well.

On a baking sheet, arrange the sweet potato slices in a single layer and bake for about 10 minutes.

Turn each chip over and bake for an additional 10 minutes, or until golden brown.

GARLIC CHIVE
HUMMUS

30 MIN + SOAKING · MAKES 4-6

1 cup dried chickpeas
soaked overnight, drained, rinsed

2 garlic cloves

4 chives roughly chopped

1 lemon juiced

¼ cup olive oil

Sea salt & black pepper to taste

In a large pot, cover your chickpeas with water and boil for about an hour.

When the chickpeas are cooked, drain and rinse. Set aside and let cool for 15–30 minutes.

Add all ingredients to a blender or food processor and blend until smooth.

Serve with slice cucumber, celery, or carrot sticks.

GRAPEFRUIT GUACAMOLE

15 MIN · MAKES 2

1 grapefruit

2 avocados chopped

½ bunch cilantro chopped

2 scallions finely chopped

½ tsp garlic powder

½ tsp cumin

Sea salt & black pepper to taste

───────────

Cut a grapefruit crossway, then use a small knife to cut each section out of the halves and add it to a large bowl.

Add the remaining ingredients and mix to your desired consistency.

Serve with chopped vegetables or flax crackers.

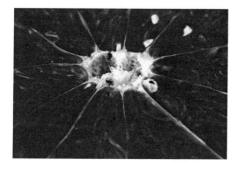

APPLES WITH ALMOND BUTTER

5 MIN · MAKES 1

1 large apple sliced

2 T almond butter for dipping

Dip apple slices in almond butter and enjoy!

BANANA "SUSHI" WITH SUNFLOWER SEED BUTTER

5 MIN · MAKES 1

1 banana peeled

¼ cup sunflower seed butter

1 T hemp seeds

———————————

Spread sunflower seed butter onto banana.

Sprinkle hemp seeds over top.

Slice and enjoy!

COOKIE DOUGH GREEK YOGURT

2 MIN · MAKES 1

1 cup vanilla Greek yogurt full-fat

1 tsp almond butter

1 T mini chocolate chips

———————

Mix ingredients together and enjoy!

ALMOND BUTTER STUFFED DATES

5 MIN · MAKES 4

4 dates

1 tsp almond butter

Pinch sea salt

———————

Cut the dates to remove the pit and spoon an even amount of nut butter into the center of each date.

Sprinkle with sea salt and enjoy!

SNACKS & SUCH

SUGAR KNOCKOUT

ROAST BEEF
& PICKLE ROLLS

5 MIN · MAKES 4-8

8 slices deli roast beef

4 pickles halved lengthwise

———————————

Wrap each pickle half in a
slice or two of deli roast beef
and enjoy!

CUCUMBER WITH
FETA & OLIVES

5 MIN · MAKES 1

1 large cucumber sliced

1 oz feta cheese

¼ cup olives

———————————

Add the ingredients to a small
bowl and enjoy!

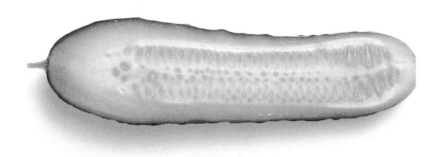

10 / SAUCES DRESSINGS CONDIMENTS

LEMON DILL VINAIGRETTE

5 MIN · MAKES 6

½ cup extra virgin olive oil

2 T apple cider vinegar

1 lemon juiced

1 garlic clove chopped

1 tsp dried dill

Sea salt & black pepper to taste

Add the ingredients to a bowl. Mix well with a fork before serving with your salad.

HOUSE BALSAMIC DRESSING

5 MIN · MAKES 12

1 cup extra virgin olive oil
first cold pressed, if possible

⅓ cup aged balsamic vinegar
high-quality

1 T dried parsley

½ tsp sea salt

Freshly ground pepper to taste

1 T honey mustard
organic, if possible

1 garlic clove minced (optional)

———————————

Add all ingredients into a bowl and whisk until thick and creamy.

Check for seasoning.

GREEK DRESSING

10 MIN · MAKES 12

¼ cup olive oil

⅓ cup red wine vinegar

2 cloves garlic minced

1 tsp dijon mustard

¾ tsp oregano

¾ tsp basil

½ tsp sea salt

½ tsp black pepper

½ tsp onion powder

———————————

Combine all ingredients into a jar or storage container and shake well.

Let the dressing sit for a minimum of 10 minutes before serving to let the flavors blend together.

CREAMY AVOCADO DRESSING

5 MIN · MAKES 12

2 avocados

½ bunch cilantro

1 lime juiced

¼ cup water

1 garlic clove

Sea salt & black pepper to taste

―――――――――――

Add all ingredients to a blender or food processor and blend until smooth.

Serve immediately.

BEET DRESSING

5 MIN · MAKES 2

2 cups beets cooked, chopped

2 T apple cider vinegar

2 T flax oil

2 T filtered water

½ tsp sea salt

———————————

Blend all ingredients on high.

Perfectly sweet, tart, and creamy—perfect over any type of greens with cucumber, red onion, and carrots. Enjoy!

SAUCES, DRESSINGS, CONDIMENTS

CHIMICHURRI SAUCE

5 MIN · MAKES 3-4

1 cup fresh flat leaf parsley

¼ cup fresh cilantro

½ cup extra virgin olive oil

⅓ cup red wine vinegar

½ tsp sea salt

2 cloves garlic

½ tsp cumin powder

½ tsp red pepper flakes

Add all ingredients to a blender or food processor and blend until smooth.

EASY MARINARA

10 MIN · MAKES 2

2 T coconut oil

3 garlic cloves chopped

28-oz can crushed tomatoes

Sea salt & black pepper to taste

————————————

Add coconut oil and garlic to a hot pan.

Sauté for about 3 minutes until brown.

Add tomatoes, sea salt & black pepper.
Simmer until hot.

SAUCES, DRESSINGS, CONDIMENTS

MANGO SALSA

5 MIN + 2 HRS · MAKES 4–6

2 mangos peeled and cubed

2 kiwi peeled and diced

1 red onion diced

1 jalapeño seeds removed, minced

1 red pepper seeds removed, diced

1 avocado peeled and diced

1 tomato diced

1 lime juiced

Bunch of cilantro chopped

½ tsp sea salt

Mix ingredients in a bowl and refrigerate for 2 hours.

Serve and enjoy!

HOMEMADE
MAYO

5 MIN · MAKES 30

1 cup olive oil

2 egg yolks free range

2 T apple cider vinegar raw

1 T lemon juice fresh

2 tsp sea salt

½ tsp mustard

⅛ tsp cayenne pepper

Set aside ¾ cup of the olive oil.

Combine remaining ingredients and blend for 30 seconds.

With blender running low, remove fill cap and drizzle reserved oil in a thin stream until mixture is thick.

Scrape into a screw-top glass jar and keep refrigerated.

Stays fresh 7–14 days.

RECIPE COURTESY OF BODY ECOLOGY

11 / DESSERTS

CHOCOLATE AVOCADO PUDDING POPS

45 MIN · MAKES 3

2 avocados

2 dates or 1 T maple syrup

2 T cocoa powder

¼ cup dairy-free milk

1 T coconut oil

1 tsp vanilla extract

Pinch of sea salt

Add all the ingredients to a blender or food processor and mix until smooth.

Pour into a popsicle mold and freeze until firm.

DESSERTS

AVOCADO ICE CREAM

10 MIN + FREEZING · MAKES 2

1 can coconut milk
refrigerated overnight

2 avocados

2 dates or stevia, to taste

_____

Blend the avocados and dates in a blender or food processor until very smooth. Pour mixture into a bowl.

Add the refrigerated coconut milk and fold into the avocado mixture with a rubber spatula.

Freeze for about 4 hours before serving.

Many raw ice cream recipes (or mostly raw, like this one) are made to be eaten the same day. If left in the freezer like conventional ice cream, the taste and texture become unappetizing.

PEANUT BUTTER
BANANA ICE CREAM

5 MIN · MAKES 1

1 frozen banana
sliced prior to freezing

⅓ cup coconut milk
or non-dairy milk of choice

1 T natural peanut butter
or chocolate chips

Blend ingredients together in a mini food processor until smooth and creamy, scraping down sides periodically.

Taste and add milk as necessary

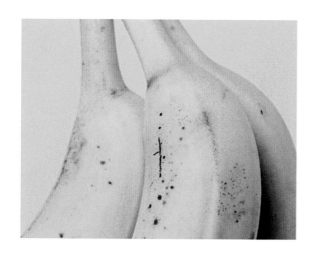

LEMON BITES

1 ½ cups almond flour

⅓ cup organic raw coconut flour

Pinch Himalayan pink salt

6 T organic liquid sweetener maple
syrup, coconut nectar,
or raw honey

⅓ cup organic lemon juice

1 T organic lemon zest

2 tsp organic vanilla extract

¼ cup organic coconut oil
melted

Shredded coconut flakes
or almond flour (optional)

Fold the dry ingredients together in
a large bowl.

Combine all wet ingredients except
coconut oil in a small bowl.

Stir the combined wet ingredients
into the dry until well mixed.

Slowly add the melted coconut oil
and mix until blended in.

Scoop a spoonful at a time and roll
into bite-sized balls.

Leave plain or roll in shredded coconut flakes or almond flour.

Chill for 20–30 minutes and keep
cold until ready to serve.

DESSERTS

SALTED CHOCOLATE COCONUT PISTACHIO CLUSTERS

40 MIN · MAKES 10-12

1 cup dark chocolate chips

1 tsp coconut extract

1 ½ cups pistachios raw

½ cup shredded coconut unsweetened

1 pinch of Himalayan pink salt

Melt chocolate in a microwave-safe bowl or double boiler.

Mix in coconut extract. Fold in pistachios.

Line a plate with parchment paper and scoop spoonfuls of the chocolate mixture onto the paper and press to flatten.

Sprinkle a tiny bit of salt and sprinkle with coconut.

Cool in freezer for at least 30 minutes to harden, and store in the refrigerator.

DARK CHOCOLATE
ALMOND MOUSSE

5 MIN + CHILLING · MAKES 5

2 cups almond milk unsweetened

½ cup chia seeds

3 T cocoa powder

⅔ cup almond butter

2 T maple syrup or raw honey

1 tsp vanilla

½ tsp salt

Blend all ingredients in a blender for 2–3 minutes until thickened, smooth and creamy.

Transfer to a bowl and refrigerate until chilled, about 3 hours. Enjoy!

TROPICAL
FAT BOMBS

60 MIN · MAKES 18

4 T coconut oil

⅓ cup raw honey

1 cup coconut butter

1 tsp vanilla

4 pieces dried mango unsweetened, chopped

¼ cup banana chips unsweetened, crushed

¼ cup coconut flakes unsweetened

In a saucepan over low heat, melt the coconut oil, honey, and coconut butter.

Add the vanilla extract and whisk until well combined.

Pour the mixture into a silicone muffin tray or muffin cups.

Top each cup with the chopped mango, banana chips, and coconut flakes.

Refrigerate one hour or until set.

12 / HOLIDAY
FAVORITES

CLASSIC TURKEY

3-4½ HOURS

12-18 lb turkey fully thawed

Sea salt & black pepper

HERB BUTTER

¾ cup unsalted butter room temperature

6 cloves garlic minced

1 tsp salt

½ tsp black pepper

1 T fresh rosemary finely chopped

1 T fresh thyme finely chopped

AROMATICS

1 onion peeled and quartered

1 lemon quartered

2 sprigs fresh rosemary

2 sprigs fresh thyme

2 sprigs fresh sage

Remove turkey from refrigerator 1 hour before roasting.

While turkey is tempering, combine herb butter ingredients in a small bowl.

Preheat oven to 325° F.

Remove giblets, season the cavity with salt and pepper, then pat-dry the skin.

Gently loosen the skin by sliding your fingers underneath it.

Rub about ⅓ of the herb butter under the skin Rub the remaining butter all over the outside of the turkey.

Add aromatics to the cavity. Don't overfill.

Place the turkey in a roasting pan and bake for 15 minutes per pound or until the internal temperature (at the thickest part of the breast) reaches 160° F.

Basting isn't necessary, but If the skin browns too quickly, tent with foil.

Let rest for 30 minutes before carving. Save drippings for gravy.

TURKEY GRAVY

20 MIN · MAKES 8

2 T butter

¼ cup gluten-free flour

3–4 cups turkey drippings
if drippings run out, use chicken stock

Sea salt & black pepper to taste

Rosemary dried, optional

Thyme dried, optional

Add butter to a large skillet and place over medium-high heat.

Once butter is melted, whisk in a little bit of flour.

Slowly add in 3 cups of drippings, alternating with the flour, whisking vigorously.

Bring the gravy to a simmer (not a boil) and allow it to thicken for a minute or two, stirring occasionally.

Add more drippings (or stock) to thin, if necessary.

Taste and add salt and pepper, if needed. Stir in dried herbs, if using.

HORSERADISH ENCRUSTED BEEF TENDERLOIN

80 MIN · MAKES 8

3 lb beef tenderloin roast

1 whole garlic bulb

1 T olive oil

⅓ cup prepared horseradish

½ tsp sea salt

¼ tsp pepper

¼ tsp dried basil

¼ tsp dried thyme

⅓ cup gluten-free bread crumbs

Remove tenderloin from refrigerator to temper, placing it on a rack in a large, shallow roasting pan.

Preheat oven to 425° F.

Remove papery outer skin from garlic bulb (do not peel or separate cloves).

Cut top off garlic bulb, coat with olive oil, and wrap in heavy-duty foil.

Bake until softened (30–35 minutes), then cool for at least 10 minutes.

Lower oven temperature to 400°.

Squeeze softened garlic into a small bowl and stir in horseradish, salt, and spices.

Add bread crumbs; stir to combine

Spread mixture over the whole tenderloin.

Bake 45–55 minutes until internal temperature reaches:

135° – medium rare
140° – medium well
145° – well done

Rest for 10 minutes before slicing.

ACORN SQUASH
& PECAN STUFFING

50 MIN · MAKES 4

28 oz acorn squash
two average-sized squash

1½ T olive oil divided

1 cup yellow onion chopped

1 tsp sea salt divided

1 cup brown or wild rice cooked

½ cup pecans toasted & chopped

½ cup dried cranberries

3 T fresh parsley chopped

2 tsp fresh sage chopped

¼ tsp black pepper

Preheat oven to 375° F.

Cut squash in half lengthwise and scoop out the seeds.

Lightly brush 1 tsp of olive oil over the open side of each piece, then place face down on a baking sheet.

Bake 30–35 minutes or until squash is wrinkled and soft.

Scoop out most of the flesh, leaving a thin border next to the skin.

Mash flesh with a fork.

Heat remaining oil in a large non-stick skillet over medium heat.

Add chopped onion and cook until it begins to soften (4–5 min).

Stir in ½ tsp of salt.

Add rice and cook until warmed through (3–4 min).

Stir in mashed squash, remaining salt, and remaining ingredients and cook for 4–6 minutes.

Spoon rice mixture into squash halves to serve. Enjoy!

HONEY GARLIC BUTTER ROASTED CARROTS

25 MIN · MAKES 6

2 lb carrots

⅓ cup grass-fed butter

3 T raw honey

4 garlic cloves minced

Sea salt & black pepper to taste

Fresh flat-leaf parsley

Preheat oven to 425° F.

Lightly grease baking sheet with about 1 tsp of butter.

Peel carrots and cut to desired length.

In a large pot, melt remaining butter and pour in honey. Stir until completely dissolved.

Add garlic and mix.

Add carrots to the pot and toss the carrots while allowing the sauce to thicken. Add salt and pepper.

Arrange the carrots in a single layer on the prepared baking sheet.

Roast for 20 minutes then garnish with parsley

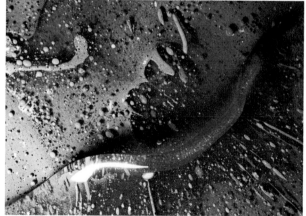

SUGAR KNOCKOUT

CRANBERRY
SAUCE

25 MIN · MAKES 10

1 bag fresh cranberries 12 oz

½ cup honey or maple syrup

½ cup water

1 orange zested, juiced

1 cinnamon stick

Combine all ingredients in a saucepan and bring to a boil.

Reduce heat and simmer for 20 minutes.

Let cool before serving.

HOLIDAY FAVORITES

SWEET POTATO CASSEROLE

45–60 MIN · MAKES 8

3 large sweet potatoes peeled and cubed

¼ cup dairy-free milk

¼ cup grass-fed butter melted

1 tsp vanilla

1 tsp cinnamon

¼ tsp nutmeg

1 tsp sea salt

¼ tsp black pepper

TOPPING

¾ cup pecans roughly chopped

¼ cup pepitas roughly chopped

4 dates pitted and diced

¼ cup almond flour

2 T butter

Bring large pot of water to a boil.

Add sweet potato chunks and cook 20–30 minutes.

Drain the potatoes and mash with a hand masher or electric beater.

Pour remaining ingredients into the sweet potatoes and mix until creamy.

Spread mixture evenly into a 9×13-inch baking dish.

Preheat oven 375° F.

Make topping: Mix dates, pecans and pepitas. Add the butter and flour, mixing thoroughly with hands until combined. Sprinkle topping onto sweet potato mixture

Bake for 25–30 minutes or until golden brown.

PUMPKIN PIE

60 MIN · MAKES 8

9-inch gluten-free crust frozen

15-oz can pumpkin

3 organic eggs

1 tsp sea salt finely ground

5 tsp pumpkin pie spice

2 T maple syrup

¾ cup coconut cream
unsweetened

———————————

Let pie crust defrost at room temperature
for 10–20 minutes.

Preheat oven 375° F.

Blend all ingredients until well incorporated and pour into pie crust.

Bake for 50–60 minutes, or until knife
inserted in the center comes out clean.

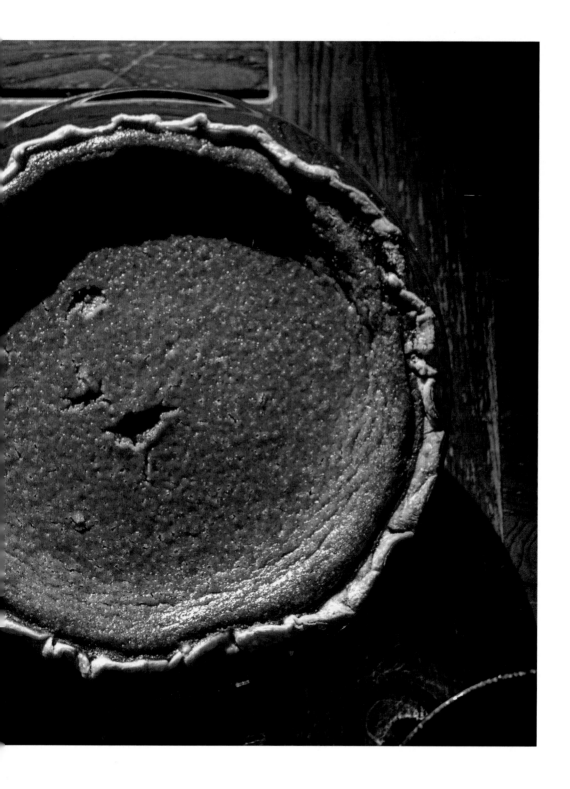

APPLE CRUMBLE

55 MIN · MAKES 8

6 apples or any fruit in season, sliced

⅓ cup honey

2 T arrow root starch

TOPPING

1 cup coconut or almond flour

1 cup cooking oats

½ tsp sea salt

½ tsp cinnamon

¼ tsp nutmeg

½ cup olive oil

⅓ cup honey

Mix apples, honey, and arrow root starch until starch dissolves and covers fruit.

Pour apples into a 9×13-inch baking dish.

Preheat over 350° F.

Make topping: Mix all dry ingredients. Add olive oil and honey, stirring to combine. Sprinkle topping onto apples.

Bake for 50 minutes or until golden brown.

MULLING SPICES

25 MIN · MAKES 8-10

3 oz cinnamon sticks
about 9 sticks

⅓ cup cardamom pods

¼ cup allspice berries

¼ cup whole cloves

¼ cup star anise

⅓ cup dried orange peel
store-bought or dried in oven

¼ cup black peppercorns

Place cinnamon sticks, cardamom pods, allspice berries, cloves, and star anise in a large Ziploc bag and seal.

Crush spices with a rolling pin to break larger spices and release oils.

Add dried orange peel and peppercorns, tossing well to mix.

HOW TO USE

Use 1–2 T spice mix per quart

Use ¼ cup per gallon

Simmer 10–20 minutes with tea, wine, cider, cranberry juice, or pomegranate juice.

Mulling spices can also be used to infuse alcohol.

SPICED HOT
CHOCOLATE

5 MIN · MAKES 1

1 cup milk (high-protein)
warmed

2–3 tsp cacao powder

1 T pure maple syrup

⅛ tsp vanilla

Pinch cinnamon

Pinch nutmeg

Pinch cayenne

Pinch sea salt

Mix all ingredients and enjoy!

POMEGRANATE SPARKLING MOCKTAIL

5 MIN · MAKES 1

3 oz pomegranate juice

1 cinnamon stick

Club soda to top off

GARNISH

Cranberries

Pomegranate seeds

Rosemary sprig

In a wine glass, add ice, pomegranate juice, and cinnamon stick.

Top off with club soda.

Garnish with cranberries, pomegranate seeds, and rosemary sprig. Enjoy!

00 / INDEX

RECIPE INDEX

INGREDIENTS INDEX

VEGETABLES

FRUIT

PROTEIN

almond butter

Apple Pie Protein Balls	129
Superfood Energy Balls	133
Apples with Almond Butter	140
Almond Butter Stuffed Dates	142
Cookie Dough Greek Yogurt	142
Dark Chocolate Almond Mousse	175

bacon

Saturday Morning Power Skillet	32

beef

Signature Steak Salad	56
Chimichurri Steak	85
Roast Beef & Pickle Rolls	144
Horseradish-Encrusted Beef	184

beef, ground

Taco Salad in a Jar	59
Easy Grass-Fed Beef Burgers	86

chicken

Chicken Minestrone	43
Chicken Tortilla Soup	44
Cream of Mushroom with Chicken	51
Slow Cooker Chicken Cacciatore	69
Go-To Chicken Salad Roll Ups	71
Ginger Chicken with Vegetables	72
Chicken Fajitas	75
Hummus Chicken	78
Chicken with Onion & Lemon	81
Cilantro Lime Chicken	82

eggs

Easy Pumpkin Pancakes	30
Peanut Butter Banana Waffles	31
Saturday Morning Power Skillet	32
Prosciutto-Wrapped Mini Muffins	34
Eggs with Tomato & Avocado	36
Turkey Sausage Scramble	37
Tofu Veggie Fried Rice	111
Homemade Mayo	160
Pumpkin Pie	194

fish

Salmon Salad	55
Tuna Salad	60
Grilled Salmon Kebabs	91
Cauliflower Mash with Salmon	95
Pan-Seared Tomato Basil Trout	97
Citrus Fish Tacos	98
Lemon Butter Halibut	101
Chipotle Salmon Burgers	102
Grilled Lime-Basil Tuna Steaks	104

lentils

Grilled Portobello Burgers	112
Red Lentil Daal with Spinach	122

pancetta

Pan-Seared Tomato Basil Trout	97

prosciutto di parma

Prosciutto-Wrapped Mini Muffins	34

protein powder

Chocolate-Covered Blueberry Smoothie	19
Easy Pumpkin Pancakes	30

salmon

Salmon Salad	55
Grilled Salmon Kebabs	91
Cauliflower Mash with Salmon	95
Chipotle Salmon Burgers	102

shrimp

Roasted Garlic Soup with Shrimp	48
Sautéed Kale with Shrimp	92

tofu

Tofu Veggie Fried Rice	111
Southwest Tofu Burrito	117
Pan-Seared Tofu with Vegetables	121

tuna

Tuna Salad	60
Grilled Lime-Basil Tuna Steaks	104

turkey

Turkey Sausage Scramble	37
Sesame Crusted Turkey	77
Classic Turkey	181
Turkey Gravy	182

SAUCES & CONDIMENTS

almond butter
Apple Pie Protein Balls	129
Superfood Energy Balls	133
Apples with Almond Butter	140
Almond Butter Stuffed Dates	142
Cookie Dough Greek Yogurt	142
Dark Chocolate Almond Mousse	175

apple cider vinegar
Lemon Cravings Blaster	12
Pan-Seared Tofu with Vegetables	121
Lemon Dill Vinaigrette	149
Homemade Mayo	160

balsamic glaze
Peach Caprese Salad	64

dijon mustard
Greek Dressing	150

honey
Lemon Cravings Blaster	12
Cranberry Flush	13
House Balsamic Dressing	150
Lemon Bites	170
Tropical Fat Bombs	176
Honey Garlic Butter Roasted Carrots	188
Cranberry Sauce	190
Apple Crumble	197

horseradish, prepared
Horseradish-Encrusted Beef	184

maple syrup
Lemon Cravings Blaster	12
Cranberry Flush	13
Vanilla Almond Overnight Quinoa	28
Grilled Salmon Kebabs	91
Pan-Seared Tofu with Vegetables	121
Maple Roasted Almonds	127
Dark Chocolate Almond Mousse	175
Cranberry Sauce	190
Pumpkin Pie	194
Spiced Hot Chocolate	201

peanut butter
Peanut Butter Banana Waffles	31
Banana w/ Sunflower Seed Butter	141
Peanut Butter Banana Ice Cream	168

salsa
Taco Salad in a Jar	59
Chipotle Salmon Burgers	102
Southwest Tofu Burrito	117
Mango Salsa	159

tahini
Winter Buddha Bowl	118

HERBS & SPICES

basil
Pan-Seared Tomato Basil Trout	97

cilantro
Smoky Lime Avocado Soup	40
Chicken Tortilla Soup	44
Black Bean Soup	47
Cilantro Lime Chicken	82
Southwest Tofu Burrito	117
Red Lentil Daal with Spinach	122
Grapefruit Guacamole	139
Creamy Avocado Dressing	152
Mango Salsa	159

chives
Cauliflower Mash with Salmon	95
Garlic Chive Hummus	136

dill
Garlic-Dill Sweet Potato Chips	135

maca powder
Superfood Energy Balls	133

nutritional yeast
Creamy Pasta with Kale	109

spirulina
Superfood Energy Balls	133

Made in the USA
Las Vegas, NV
23 September 2024

65ab62bd-b186-402d-aaa0-0448e138afe0R02